mis fiestas · my celebrations

George Ancona

With Alma Flor Ada and F. Isabel Campoy
Language Consultants

Children's Press® A Division of Scholastic Inc.
New York · Toronto · London · Auckland · Sydney · Mexico City · New Delhi · Hong Kong · Danbury, Connecticut

To Katherine Breen

Thanks to the people who helped me to produce this book:
Jeanette Castillo and her children, José and Kassandra; Monica Tavares and
Monica Armendariz of the El Museo del Barrio in New York; Ellen Braaf,
Gustavo Gutierrez and Julia García of the Comité Pro Boliviano; Chris Williams
of the office of Heritage Arts in Arlington, Virginia; Luis Abea of the Martin
Luther King School; Emma Vergara and her boys, Cristóbal and Washington,
in Los Angeles; Zofía Trujillo, Seamus Alessio, and their families and
Kathy and Lance Chilton of Albuquerque, New Mexico.

Gracias,
G.A.

Library of Congress Cataloging-in-Publication Data

Ancona, George.
  Mis fiestas = My celebrations / George Ancona.
        p. cm. — (Somos latinos)
  Parallel Spanish and English text.
  Includes bibliographical references and index.
  ISBN 0–516–25290–9 (lib.bdg.)   0–516–25497–9 (pbk.)
 1. Festivals—Latin America. 2. Holidays—Latin America. 3. Latin America—Social life and customs.
 I. Title: My festivals. II. Title.
  GT4813.5.A53 2005
  394.26—dc22

                                        2005000352

Published in 2005 by Children's Press, an imprint of Scholastic Library Publishing.
Published simultaneously in Canada.
Printed in the United States of America.
1 2 3 4 5 6 7 8 9 10 R 14 13 12 11 10 09 08 07 06 05

Contenido • Contents

En toda América Latina se celebran fiestas parecidas, pero cada país tiene un modo especial de celebrarlas. Algunas de estas fiestas son: el Día de Reyes, el Día de la Independencia, el Día de los Muertos y las Navidades. Cuatro niños, José, Valeria, Cristóbal y Zofía, nos muestran cómo celebran estas fiestas aquí en los Estados Unidos.

La familia de José vino de Puerto Rico. Los padres de Valeria vinieron de Bolivia. Cristóbal vino ha de Ecuador. Y miembros de la familia de Zofía fueron de los primeros españoles que se asentaron en el Suroeste hace un largo tiempo. Estas fiestas no sólo son importantes para las personas que hablan español, sino también para sus vecinos que se unen a sus celebraciones.

Many of the same festivals are celebrated in Latin America, but each country does it in its own way. Some of these special days are: Three Kings Day, Independence Day, the Day of the Dead, and Christmas. Four children, José, Valeria, Cristóbal, and Zofía, show us how they celebrate these holidays here in the United States.

José's family came from Puerto Rico. Valeria's parents came from Bolivia. Cristóbal's came from Ecuador. And Zofía's family members were early settlers from Spain in the Southwest. These holidays are important not only to Spanish-speaking people, but also to their neighbors who join them in their celebrations.

Yo soy José. Para el Día de los Reyes Magos dejo heno y agua para los camellos de los Reyes. Por la mañana, tres hombres vestidos de reyes abren el desfile. Por las calles se ven muñecos gigantes que representan a los Reyes.

I am José. For Three Kings Day I put out hay and water for the three kings' camels. In the morning, three men dressed as the kings lead a parade. Giant puppets of the kings are rolled along.

EL MUSEO

Aquí vienen los tres reyes, Baltasar, Gaspar, y Melchor.

Here come the three kings, Balthazar, Caspar, and Melchior.

Viene gente de toda la ciudad para celebrar. Muchas personas se disfrazan para unirse al desfile. Los niños hacen y decoran coronas de papel y ven pasar a los Reyes.

People come from all over the city to celebrate. Many people dress up in costumes to join the parade. Kids make and decorate paper crowns and watch the kings go by.

Hola, soy Valeria. Nosotros celebramos el Día de la Independencia de Bolivia con bailes y música. Nuestro baile viene de una región llamada Yungas, donde había muchas personas africanas que fueron esclavizadas.

Hi, I am Valeria. We celebrate our Bolivian Independence Day with dances and music. Our dance is from the place called Yungas, where there were many enslaved Africans.

Cada grupo de danzantes representa una región de Bolivia. Algunos se visten como los habitantes de la cordillera, mientras que otros se visten como las personas de los valles y las ciudades.

Each group of dancers represents a different region of Bolivia. Some dress as they do in the mountains, while others dress like the people in the valleys and cities.

Many groups wear masks. Because people came to Bolivia from other parts of the world, the costumes honor those who came from Africa and Europe.

Muchos grupos usan máscaras. A Bolivia llegaron personas de otras partes del mundo. Los trajes recuerdan a los que vinieron de África y de Europa.

Me llamo Cristóbal. Mi hermano se llama Washington. En Los Ángeles celebramos el Día de los Muertos. Construimos altares donde ponemos fotos de personas que han muerto rodeadas con velas, flores, frutas y pan.

My name is Cristóbal. My brother's name is Washington. In Los Angeles we celebrate the Day of the Dead. We make altars where we put pictures of people who have died surrounded by candles, flowers, fruit, and bread.

Nos maquillamos o nos ponemos caretas para parecer calaveras. Luego vamos por el barrio para ver obras de teatro y de títeres que se burlan de la muerte.

We put on makeup or masks that look like skulls. We then go out in the neighborhood to see plays and puppet shows that make fun of death.

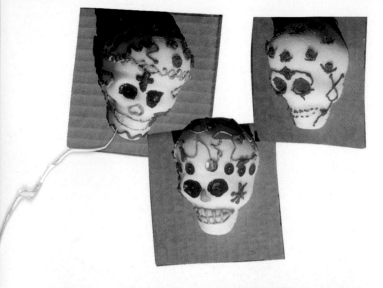

Una de las cosas que más me gusta es hacer calaveras de azúcar y decorarlas. Luego nos las comemos. También decoramos nuestros altares con papel picado y títeres de esqueletos.

One of my favorite things that we do is make sugar skulls and decorate them. We can eat them later! We also make skeleton puppets and paper cutouts to decorate our altars.

Soy Zofía. Este año me eligieron para representar a María en Las Posadas. Mi amigo Seamus hace de José. Al anochecer hacemos una procesión por el barrio y los amigos y vecinos llevan velas y cantan.

I'm Zofía. This year I was asked to be Mary in *Las Posadas*. My friend Seamus will be Joseph. When it gets dark outside we have a procession through the neighborhood with friends who carry candles and sing.

Nos detenemos a cantar en nueve casas. En la última casa abren la puerta y nos dejan entrar. Después de comer, nos vamos al patio a romper una piñata.

We stop at nine houses to sing. At the last house, we are invited in. After dinner, we go out to the backyard and break a *piñata*.

La historias de la familia

Los abuelos de José vinieron de Puerto Rico. La madre de José mantiene las tradiciones. En Navidad deja el arbolito hasta el Día de los Reyes.

Los padres de Valeria vinieron de Bolivia. Su padre creció en la ciudad de Cochabamba, en la cordillera de los Andes. Además de hablar español e inglés, también habla quechua, el idioma de los indígenas de los Andes.

La familia de Cristóbal vino de Ecuador. Al celebrar el Día de los Muertos, honran y recuerdan a sus familiares que han muerto aquí y en Ecuador.

La familia del padre de Zofía ha vivido aquí por muchas generaciones. Siguen hablando español y mantienen las tradiciones de sus antepasados que llegaron desde España. La familia de su madre vino de Irlanda y de Francia.

Family Histories

José's grandparents came from Puerto Rico. His mother keeps their traditions. For Christmas she keeps the tree up until Three Kings Day.

Valeria's parents came from Bolivia. Her father grew up in Cochabamba, a city in the Andes Mountains. In addition to Spanish and English, he also speaks Quechua, a language spoken in the Andes.

Cristóbal's family came from Ecuador. By celebrating the Day of the Dead, they honor and remember their dead relatives here and in Ecuador.

Zofía's father's family has been here for many generations. They still speak Spanish and keep their family traditions from Spain. Her mother's family came from Ireland and France.

UNITED STATES

New York City, NY

Arlington, VA

Los Angeles, CA
•Albuquerque., NM

SPAIN

North

West ○ East

South

MEXICO

CUBA

DOMINICAN
REPUBLIC

PACIFIC
OCEAN

BELIZE

HAITI

PUERTO RICO

ATLANTIC
OCEAN

AFRICA

GUATEMALA
EL SALVADOR
HONDURAS
NICARAGUA
COSTA RICA
PANAMA

Caribbean Sea

VENEZUELA

0   1000 miles

COLOMBIA

0   1000 kilometers

ECUADOR

PERU

BRAZIL

BOLIVIA

Países donde se habla español
Countries where Spanish is spoken

PARAGUAY

El viaje de la familia de José
José's Family's Journey

El viaje de la familia de Valeria
Valeria's Family's Journey

CHILE

El viaje de la familia de Cristóbal
Cristóbal's Family's Journey

ARGENTINA

URUGUAY

El viaje de la familia de Zofía
Zofía's Family's Journey

Bolivia fue bautizada así por Simón
   Bolívar quien logró la independencia
   de la América del Sur.
España fue el primer país que colonizó
   gran parte del continente americano.
Puerto Rico es parte del Commonwealth de
   los Estados Unidos.
Ecuador está cruzado por la línea del ecuador.

Bolivia is named after Simón Bolívar who won
   the independence of South America.
Spain was the first nation to colonize a major
   part of the Western Hemisphere.
Puerto Rico is part of the Commonwealth of the
   United States.
The equator runs through the country of Ecuador.

Sobre Fiestas Latina

Los pueblos de América Latina son muy distintos unos de otros. Antes de la llegada de los europeos el hemisferio occidental estaba ya habitado por gentes de culturas, lenguas y religiones diferentes. Sus festivales honraban a sus dioses y a sus cosechas; la tierra, los cielos y el agua y todo lo que vive y muere. Luego vinieron gentes desde Europa, África y Asia y estas culturas se entremezclaron con las tradiciones autóctonas. Podemos ver, oír y saborear las diferencias de la gran variedad de los países de habla hispana a través de sus fiestas.

About Latin Festivals

The people of Latin America are varied. Even before the Europeans came, the entire Western Hemisphere was filled with different cultures, languages, and religions. Their festivals honored their gods and harvests; the earth, skies and water; and all that lives and dies. Then came people from Europe, Asia, and Africa, and these cultures blended with the native traditions. We can see, hear, and taste the differences in the festivals of the many Spanish-speaking nations.

Fiestas Latinas

A través de América Latina, cada pueblo o ciudad celebra el día de su santo patrón o patrona. Estos son otros días de fiesta:

1 de enero, **Año Nuevo**

6 de enero, **Día de los Reyes Magos**

1 de mayo, **Día de los Trabajadores**

5 de mayo, **Cinco de Mayo (México)**

24 de julio, **Día de Simón Bolívar (Ecuador)**

6 de agosto, **Día de la Independencia de Bolivia**

16 de septiembre, **Día de la Independencia de México**

12 de octubre, **Día de la Raza**

21 de octubre, **Festival del Cristo Negro (Panamá)**

1 de noviembre, **Todos los Santos**

2 de noviembre, **Día de los Muertos**

25 de diciembre, **Navidad**

Latin Festivals

Throughout Latin America, each town and city celebrates its own patron saint. Here are a few other festivals:

January 1, **New Year's Day**

January 6, **Three Kings Day**

May 1, **Labor Day**

May 5, **Cinco de Mayo (Mexico)**

July 24, **Simón Bolívar Day (Ecuador)**

August 6, **Bolivian Independence Day**

September 16, **Mexican Independence Day**

October 12, **Columbus Day**

October 21, **Black Christ Festival (Panama)**

November 1, **All Saints' Day**

November 2, **Day of the Dead**

December 25, **Christmas**

Palabras en español = Words in English

burro, burra	=	donkey
calavera	=	skull
corona	=	crown
disfraz	=	costume
elegante	=	fancy
esclavo	=	slave
esqueleto	=	skeleton
heno	=	hay
maquillaje	=	makeup
máscara, careta	=	mask
parada, desfile	=	parade
títere, muñeco	=	puppet
vela	=	candle

Índice

Index

Sobre el autor

A George Ancona le gustan las fiestas. Hacer este libro fue una gran celebración. Cuando más feliz se siente es cuando pasea entre el jolgorio de la gente, observando a los que bailan, escuchando la música y husmeando el aroma de la variedad de comidas que se asan en las parrillas. Por medio de la fotografía, George ha recorrido el mundo en un viaje de descubrimiento personal. Y cuando levanta la cámara para hacer una foto, suele encontrarse con una gran sonrisa en la cara de las gentes.

About the Author

George Ancona loves to celebrate. Doing this book was a labor of love. He is happiest when he wanders through crowds of merrymakers, watches the dancers, listens to the music, and smells the aroma of different foods sizzling on the grills. Through photography, he has traveled around the world on a personal trip of discovery. And when he lifts his camera to take a picture, most people greet him with a big smile.

Sobre Alma Flor Ada y F. Isabel Campoy

Alma Flor e Isabel son buenas amigas de George. Cuando lo visitan en Santa Fé les gusta ir a descubrir las pastelerías y sentarse a tomar un chocolate caliente, mientras ríen y hablan de libros. Ellas son autoras de muchos libros para niños y jóvenes, en los que hablan de la riqueza de la cultura hispana.

About Alma Flor Ada and F. Isabel Campoy

Alma Flor and Isabel are good friends of George. When they visit him in Santa Fé they like to go on the search of good bakeries, where they can have hot chocolate, laugh, and talk about books. They are authors of many books for children and young adults in which they talk about the richness of their Hispanic culture.